Parents Guidebook for Traveling with Children by Plane

Estelle Kramer and Victoria E. Waller

Disney Press

NEW YORK

To my grandchildren—Abel, Eli, Amy, Sarah,
Hannah, and Adam
—E. K.
To Marshall, Andrew, and Alison, with all my love
—V. W.

FIRST EDITION

1 3 5 7 9 10 8 6 4 2

ISBN: 1-56282-117-2

Contents

Introduction

My Disney Busy Bag for *Traveling with Children by Plane* was designed to provide activities to make traveling with children ages three to six as pleasant and successful as possible. Because each child is unique and each situation different, every traveling pitfall cannot be anticipated. Included within this guidebook for parents are solutions to some of the most common problems encountered by families on the go. Each section is short and easy to read and can be referred to again and again when you need information on playing with your children, making reservations, getting ready to go, talking to your children before the trip, packing, time spent on the plane, arriving at your destination, the return trip home, and suggested books for you to read with your children, both to prepare them for travel and to occupy them while on the trip. The calendar at the back of this book can be used not only to plan your family's travels but also to keep a log of all the places you visit while you are away from home.

Below are some explanations and hints for using the various components of this **My Disney Busy Bag.**

Activity cards come in a reusable envelope and are intended for parents to read and use with their children in the airport, on the plane, or while on the go. The games and other activities encourage active listening, observation, and critical thinking—laying the groundwork for kids to build strong communication and reasoning skills. Each activity helps children grow in different areas, from learning simple classification and determination of relationships to developing basic math skills. Activity cards create a positive environment for parents and children to communicate through play, having fun together while children learn.

The two activity cards containing finger plays are good for quick mood changes when your children are getting nervous or bored, allowing them to exercise their muscles after sitting on the plane for long periods at a time. Finger plays are more than just silly games; they help children learn to pay attention to specific instructions, and they are often a child's first opportunity to participate in the telling of a story through more than just words.

Each of the five Disney character picture cards is keyed to a specific activity card and is intended to be used by the child, either alone or with a parent. All of the questions were designed to encourage communication between you and your children. Encourage them to make up stories about each picture. Some pictures may spark your children's imagination more than others, but the important thing is that your children feel good about thinking creatively. There are no right or wrong answers. Some of the questions on the corresponding activity cards are specific, asking "How many flowers do you see?" or "What in this picture is red?" But some of the questions are less exact, requiring more creative thinking, such as "What would you plant in a garden?" or "What is the funniest thing in this picture?" Still others are interpretive and require your kids to take an image from the picture and follow it through to one of its next logical stages, asking "Who do you think lives in this house?" or "Where do you think Clarabelle will go in her yellow dress?"

Children ages three to six are already beginning to learn the names of the city, state or province, and country in which they live. All the continents on the write-on/wipe-off map of the world are individual colors, except North America. This was done to enable you and your kids to more easily identify the United States and Canada. There are many activities you and your children can share using this map. Some suggestions are included on the activity card entitled Map of the United States and Canada. You can compare the sizes of the different continents and ask other questions to encourage your children's powers of observation. These activities will increase your children's vocabulary, pique their curiosity, and help them develop a basic awareness of geography.

The blank *My Trip* book has as many uses as your kids can imagine. It may be used like any other drawing book or diary, or you can encourage your children to use it as a scrapbook of your family's travels by attaching photographs, postcards, menus, napkins, place mats, or programs to it and by drawing pictures of their favorite sights from the trip.

Sewing cards help develop children's hand-eye and muscle coordination and stretch their attention spans by giving them an activity that requires time and patience yet is enjoyable and fun. The younger your children, the harder it will be for them to keep the yarn inside the card holes, so be prepared for some crazy stitches. Help your children if they ask for help, but remember to provide positive reinforcement—even if most of the stitches go around the card. It takes time and larger hands to sew "correctly" on the cards.

Hello World is a full-color book that explores the cities of the world with Mickey Mouse and his friends. Read it for enjoyment if you are traveling domestically; international travelers may wish to talk about the places they will visit, using the book as a guide. After reading the book with your children, you may want to let them look through it and make up stories to go with the pictures. Reading with your kids is not only a special way to spend time together but will extend your children's vocabulary and language skills, encourage them to use their imagination, and introduce them to the world outside your home.

Playing with Your Children

Children ages three to six learn through play. Play encourages creativity and language and reasoning skills. The activities in this **My Disney Busy Bag** were designed for parents and children to do together and can also be used by children alone during quiet playtimes.

It is important to build children's self-esteem. When playing with your kids, be sure to praise them. Children who are rewarded with praise for trying are more likely to try again. If they are frequently criticized, they may be reluctant to attempt new things. Statements such as "Great idea," "Nice try," "Terrific," and "I like all the colors you used" encourage children. Successful play experiences set up a pattern for future success, both in and out of school.

When playing with your children, remember that each child is unique. Some children catch on to things quickly, whereas others may need more explanation. If your child cannot grasp a particular activity, put it away and select another. Be patient and try not to show disappointment.

Parents frequently take over their children's play by bringing their own ideas to the games and activities. This can limit parent-child interaction, inhibit children's imaginations, and make children feel less in control of their play. Give your kids a chance to lead the way during playtime, and they will often surprise you with their creativity. Be respectful of your children's wishes—they don't need to "finish" a game, picture card, or drawing in order to have fun or to enjoy your time together.

Reservations

Families with children have specific needs when traveling, and meeting them is often just a matter of making a phone call or two. Reservations made well in advance will help turn a trip into a carefree adventure. This section offers suggestions for making airline, airport shuttle, car rental, and hotel reservations.

You can make airline reservations either by calling the airline directly (all major airlines have toll-free numbers) or by calling a travel agent. A travel agent can also make your hotel and car rental arrangements, as well as provide you with much of the literature you may want before leaving.

Tell the travel or ticketing agent the ages of your children; there are often promotional fares for children up to age seventeen. There may also be a special rate for adults traveling with kids.

The agent can also advise you when the route is least crowded—something to think about when traveling with small children, because a plane with fewer passengers will allow you more overhead storage room and perhaps more than one seat for each of you. Take into consideration the best time of day or night for your children to travel. Some kids will sleep on a plane; others will not. Plan to return home a day or two before work or school begins to give you and your children time to get back into your regular schedule.

Before making your travel reservations, give some thought to where you'd like to sit on the plane. Ask whether there are one or two aisles on the plane and how many seats are in each row. Most kids prefer looking out the window to sitting on the aisle, so if you are traveling with more than one child, you may want to request seats in a few rows so you will have more window seats available. Try to minimize any advance discussion with children about seat assignments, because you never know exactly where your seats will be until you are on the plane.

Bulkhead seats are the first seats in any section of the plane. There are no other passengers seated directly in front of them. These seats usually offer more leg room and are sometimes close to the bathrooms, which make them appealing to those traveling with children. Keep in mind, however, that all carry-on luggage must be stored in the overhead compartment and that the armrests—which usually lift up in other seats—cannot be removed.

When making reservations, be sure to ask how many pieces of carry-on baggage are permitted and what size they should be. Try to get your boarding passes when you purchase your tickets: Waiting on one less line at the airport means one less hassle for your family.

At this time you should also ask what meals will be served on your flights and what special meals are available. Unless just a snack will be served, you can order one of several special meals for yourself or your kids. Most airlines offer some selection of special meals for babies, toddlers, and children; meals for those with dietary restrictions, such as diabetic, low sodium, low calorie, low cholesterol/low fat, and bland; as well as kosher, vegetarian, fruit plate, and hot or cold seafood, among others.

Now is also the time to decide how you will get to and from the airport. Whether you ask a friend to drive you, arrange for an airport van, or park your car in the long-term lot at the airport, early planning will spare you some last-minute anxiety. If someone is picking you up at the airport (upon arrival either at your destination or at home), designate a meeting place—such as the gate or baggage claim area—ahead of time, to avoid confusion. If you plan to take an airport van, reserve your places as early as possible and be sure to reconfirm them at least twenty-four hours before your flight. Call the airport for information about long-term parking and remember to leave yourself extra time to find a parking space on the day of your departure.

Motels, hotels, all-suite hotels (some of which have kitchens in the rooms), bed-and-breakfast inns, and campsites are just some of the accommodations available to families on the go. When making reservations, ask about special rates for children, as well as holiday or weekend rates, if applicable. Comparison shop to find out what family packages are available. Remember to ask about luxury, state, and city taxes and whether there is a charge for parking. Charges such as these can add a lot to the cost of what may at first seem like a bargain.

Be sure to find out the specifics about sleeping arrangements at this point. Find out how many beds are in each room, what size they are, and whether rollaway cots or cribs are also available. If you know you'll be needing a cot or a crib, reserve it now; most facilities have only a limited number available. Some hotels have connecting rooms, which are a good idea when traveling with several children.

Ask about check-in and check-out times and find out what services are available for your family if you arrive before your room is ready. You may want to store your bags, be able to freshen up, or change into your bathing suits while you wait. This would also be a good time to ask if the room is guaranteed for late arrival.

Find out if there's a playground, a pool, or a program of organized activities for children: Many hotels have special programs for families during holidays and over the summer. Ask the management to send you any printed materials or brochures, which you can use to help prepare your children for the trip. Ask about nearby family restaurants, movie theaters, and other local attractions. Sometimes the hotel can send you brochures or guide you to someone who can. Find out if the hotel offers baby-sitting services. (Adults might want to go out alone one night, giving the children a chance to eat and watch TV in the room—a welcome break for everyone.) Finally, ask whether there are laundry facilities on (or nearby) the premises and whether the hotel can provide transportation to and from the airport.

There are additional considerations when you plan to stay with friends or at a bed and breakfast. If you are staying with friends or relatives, children may have to sleep on a sofa bed or share a room with your hosts' children. If you will be at a bed and breakfast, the bathroom may be down the hall. You should give your kids as much information as you can to help them prepare for the trip. Determine the logistics of your stay (such as sleeping arrangements and what pets, if any, your hosts have) so you will be able to discuss them with your children ahead of time.

If you plan to rent a car or van at your destination, make sure to make your reservations as soon as you know your flight information. This is especially crucial if you will be traveling at busy times of the year, such as during a school vacation or holiday. Check for special rates or discounts through the airline, your automobile club, and any other organization to which you may belong. An advertised or quoted price is often the base price, so inquire about what additional costs there may be for insurance, emergency road assistance, or extra mileage. Some credit card companies and auto insurance policies provide rental car insurance; knowing this ahead of time can save you money.

When making your reservation, specify the type of car or van you want. There is usually a great deal of luggage when traveling with young kids, so make sure the trunk of the car you'll be renting is large enough for your needs. Ask about the availability of car seats and what the additional charges will be. These fees vary (from $2 to $20 per day), so be sure to check around. Remember to request the car seats when making your reservations.

Reserve a car after you have booked your family's airline tickets, so you will be able to give the agent your flight number and arrival time. Confirm that the on-site facility at your destination will be open when you arrive. Always get a confirmation number and the name of the agent with whom you make your reservations.

Again: Call a day before your departure to reconfirm all reservations.

Getting Ready to Go

There are some basic preparations to help make your family plane trip worry free and enjoyable. The following is a list of some of the more important things to remember during the planning stages of your trip:

1. As soon as you have decided where you are going, write to the chamber of commerce in each area you plan to visit and ask them to send brochures and pamphlets about local activities and sights. These will help you and your children plan the details of your days away from home. They are a good tool for getting your children involved in the trip preparations. Many theme parks, museums, and other attractions can also send you printed materials. Call or write for them as early as possible.

2. If this will be your children's first experience on a plane, take them to the airport a week or

two before your flight. Talk about the planes and tell them what a flight is like, stressing the positive, fun aspects of air travel.

3. Use the calendar provided at the back of this guidebook to plan your time away from home. You can begin by showing your children what day they should have their own tote bags packed and ready, when their last day of school is, and when they'll be coming home.

4. In the space provided at the back of this guidebook, list the phone numbers of your airline(s), rental car agency, and hotel(s) in which you'll be staying, the names of the people with whom you speak, and your flight and confirmation numbers.

5. Tell your neighbors that you will be away and give them a copy of your itinerary so they can reach you in an emergency. You might also want to leave them the name and number of a close relative. Note your neighbors' phone numbers in the back of this book in case you need to contact them for any reason.

6. Be sure to have supplies and nonperishable foods—such as diapers, clean towels and sheets, and a well-stocked freezer and cupboard—in your home for your return.

Talking to Your Children Before the Trip

You should start talking about the trip with your children one or two weeks before you plan to leave. Telling children too soon can result in endless questions about when you will be leaving. Explain that they will be flying on a plane, visiting different places, not sleeping in their own bed, and eating in restaurants. You can talk about where you are going, what you plan to do there, and how you are getting there. Children feel important when they are included in the plans; this is, after all, a *family* trip.

If you will be visiting friends or relatives and plan to stay in their home, you should talk with your kids about who lives in the house. Tell your kids that you expect them to follow the house rules and behave themselves. If you have photos of the people you are going to visit, show them to your children.

Some children may ask specific questions or want reassurance about a particular fear, such as leaving behind a family pet. Try to answer their questions as honestly as you can and remember that leaving home for any period of time—even with the family—can be an overwhelming experience for very young children. Emphasize that family travel is a fun adventure.

Packing

When packing for an entire family, organization is of the utmost importance. From the moment you begin planning your trip, keep a running list of everything you and your children will need. This will lessen the likelihood of forgetting necessary items. The list below is a good place to start. Use the checklist and the space provided in the back of this book to list all of your family's specifics.

1. Mark all the suitcases you will be checking through on the plane so they can be easily spotted on the baggage carousel. Ribbons, pom-poms, or colored masking tape are helpful in distinguishing your family's luggage.
2. In addition to having a luggage tag on each piece of baggage, make sure to put your name inside each suitcase in case the tag comes off.

3. Label all of the items you carry, including strollers, camera bags, children's totes, and diaper totes.

4. Take one suitcase for each child; if two kids are sharing the same suitcase, divide it and keep the children's clothes separate in each half.

5. Bringing along a child's own pillow and blanket and a plug-in night-light help make a strange bedroom seem more familiar.

6. Pack some extra plastic bags to fill with laundry, wet bathing suits, seashells, and anything else you might want to keep separate while traveling.

7. The type of clothing you pack depends on the weather of the area to which you will be traveling. In addition to the appropriate seasonal clothing, you should also bring a lightweight shirt or two, even when traveling to cold places. Layering clothes not only helps retain body heat but also allows for removal of outer layers when interior spaces become overly hot. Similarly, a sweater may be invaluable when visiting warmer areas that are excessively air conditioned. Easy-to-carry rain gear will come in handy when planning all-day excursions, as the weather

may vary greatly throughout the course of a day. A day or two before you leave, you might want to check the newspaper weather listings for the area you'll be visiting.

8. When packing for children, take clothes that are washable and dark and won't show dirt quickly.

9. Bring plenty of underwear so you won't have to wash them out every night.

10. Make sure that each child has at least one pair of shoes or sneakers that are comfortable for walking.

11. Each child should have a tote bag containing a few of his or her favorite books and toys. It should be small enough for the children to carry on their own, but don't expect them to carry it all the time. Encourage your kids to be responsible for their bag and to always keep track of where it is. This tote can be used in the airport and on the plane, as well as in the hotel room. Let your children choose which toys and books to bring. The books should be ones that the kids can look at alone when you are busy. If your children sleep with or have a fondness for a particular blanket or stuffed animal, make sure to carry it aboard the plane. Choose toys

carefully: Select only those with no small pieces or irreplaceable parts and do not pack musical instruments or other noisy toys. Separate the toys that are to be used on the plane from those specifically for the hotel. The ones for the hotel can be packed in one of the suitcases to be checked in at the air-port. You may want to include a bathtub toy or two in one of the checked suitcases.

12. Pack a small bag for yourself to carry onto the plane and throughout your family's trav-els. This adult tote should contain a folding umbrella, a flashlight, a camera, film, extra batteries, a small sewing kit, a small pocket knife, tissues, adhesive bandages, sun block, hats, and fever and pain relievers. Re-member to bring any medications that you or your children take regularly. If any of you have a history of certain illnesses and re-spond well to a specific antibiotic, take it with you.

13. Bring aboard a sweater for each child, in case the plane is very cold, and a change of clothes in case of accidents.

14. Be prepared for the possibility of lost lug-gage by packing a carry-on bag with paja-mas, toothbrushes, toothpaste, and other

items your family might need the first night of your trip.

15. Although food is served on almost all airline flights, unexpected delays can sometimes mean going for long periods without eating. Pack some small, easy-to-eat, nonperishable snacks—nothing juicy, sticky, or too sugary—such as drink boxes, small boxes of cereal, crackers, sandwiches, and cut-up fruit in lidded containers. Gum and sucking candies can be used during takeoff and landing to relieve any pressure on the ears.

16. If anyone in your family wears glasses, take along the prescription or an extra pair in case they break. Always carry your health insurance cards and make sure to list your family physician's phone number in the back of this guidebook.

At the Airport

When checking your luggage (whether at the curbside checking area or inside the terminal), double-check that the bags are being sent to the right place. Lost luggage, always a hassle, is made more complicated by the extra worries of traveling with children.

Before boarding the plane, take the kids to the bathroom. This will eliminate the possibility of their needing to use the airplane lavatory while other passengers are still boarding.

On the Plane

Families with children are given the opportunity to board the plane ahead of other passengers. These extra few minutes will help you get your children settled into their seats and familiarize them with the plane. As you board, tell the flight attendant your family's name and seat assignments. This should expedite service of special meals. Ask the flight attendant if any playing cards or games are available for your kids. Request a cup of ice chips for each child to suck. Sucking on the chips is a good substitute for gum or candy to keep ears from popping during takeoff.

Put your carry-on baggage in the compartments above the seats and remove the pillows and blankets. Place the items that you will use often during the flights—including your child's tote and the snacks—under the seat in front of you. Even if you are sitting in the bulkhead, where you can keep only small items on your seat until after the plane is airborne, keep each child's favorite toy with them.

Once you are all seated, make sure there is an airsickness bag in the pocket of the seat in front of you. Explain to your children what each of the buttons on the side of their seat or above them does. If you have a window seat, look out the window and point out the other planes and the baggage handlers moving the luggage. Talk about where the suitcases are put, where the pilots sit, what the flight attendants do, where the meals are made and stored, and where the bathrooms are.

As people enter the plane, explain airplane rules to your children—no kicking the seat in front of them, no climbing on their seat, no bothering other passengers by yelling or peering over the tops of the seats, and no playing with lap trays. Remind your kids that, just as in a car, safety belts are to be worn at all times.

After everyone has boarded, talk about what will happen next. The flight attendant will address the passengers about plane safety, and then the pilot will make an announcement. Create a game by asking your kids to watch the signs that say No Smoking and Fasten Your Seat Belt and to tell you when they go on and off.

Introduce the word *turbulence* in case it occurs midflight. Explain that turbulence is air that isn't smooth and that causes some bumpiness. Compare this to riding over a bumpy street near your home or to riding in the back of a bus. Mention the noise that the plane will make when it takes off and lands and let your kids know that their ears may feel funny at those times. Practice chewing and swallowing and tell the children this will help unclog their ears. If the pressure creates unbearable pain for one of your children, and he or she cries, don't become flustered or angry. The passengers around you will understand. The most you can do in such cases is to tell your child it will be over soon, encourage him or her to keep swallowing and chewing, and offer comfort. Try to distract your child by telling a story or reading a book out loud.

After the plane is airborne, you can lift or remove the armrest between your seats. This will give you and your children more room and comfort.

When you take your child to the bathroom, remember that on some planes the noise of flushing can be frightening. Open the door and let your child out before flushing.

Should your child need to throw up, you can

help by reassuring him or her that everything will be all right, and that you will stay right there. Ask the flight attendant to bring your child some cola or club soda to sip. This is an instance in which having a change of clothes handy can be very helpful.

If another child on the plane starts to cry and this agitates your kids, reassure them that the child's parents are taking care of him or her, just as you are there to take care of your own children.

Timid fliers should try not to make their children fearful. Use the time on the plane to cuddle, read a story, and play games. These activities will keep you busy and help calm your anxieties. You might want to rent headsets from the flight attendant, so everyone can sit back, relax, and listen to music or watch a movie, if one is offered.

The pilot will usually make announcements as you approach your destination, or you can ask the flight attendant to let you know when the plane is about half an hour from landing. Make sure your children have something to chew (or more ice) before the descent begins. Talk about the landing and the bump the plane makes as it touches the ground. If relatives or friends are meeting you, tell your kids who will be at the airport. Reassure your children that you will stay close by to help them meet the unfamiliar faces. Give the kids time to finish playing and put all their toys away before the plane lands.

After landing, gather all your belongings from under the seats and the overhead compartments. It is often easier to deplane once all the other passengers have already done so.

At the Destination

Remind children to stay close to you at the airport. Stop at the rest rooms on the way to the baggage claim area.

When picking up your rental car, make sure to check for a spare tire, emergency repair kit, and that seats, lights, and windshield wipers are in working order. Ask the agent to give you both a map of the city and directions back from your hotel to the car drop-off location at the airport.

By the time you arrive at the hotel, each adult should have a predetermined set of responsibilities. If one adult looks after the children and the baggage while the other checks in and gets the room keys, the process will go much more smoothly. If your room is not available immediately and you want to leave your bags at the front desk, make sure to count them and check that each has a name tag.

Once you get into your room, check balconies and doors. A balcony door that can be opened easily is a potential danger. Make it clear to the kids that some areas—such as balconies, hallways, and elevators—are off limits without an adult present. Check fire exits and plug in your night-light.

Whether you are staying in a hotel or with friends or relatives, remind your children to be especially considerate.

If you have had an exhausting day of travel or sightseeing, let the children sleep late the next morning. You'll all have a better day if the kids are well rested. Everyone needs to relax while away from home.

International Travel

When planning international family travel, allow yourself a few months to get your children's passports and to find out whether you require visas or immunizations for the countries you will be visiting. Your family physician may be able to provide a list of English-speaking doctors in the areas to which you will be traveling. Bring along extra passport-size photos and a photocopy of each person's passport. Store them separately from the originals in case of loss or theft.

International flights are usually long and some children will have difficulty sleeping on them. This makes it even more important to make sure everyone is comfortable.

As the plane approaches your destination, discuss with your children what will occur once they leave the plane. Explain that people will be speaking a foreign language and reassure your kids that you will stay by their side.

For security reasons, there may be armed soldiers at some foreign airports. Ask the flight attendant if this will be the case when you land. If so, tell the children that the soldiers are like police officers who are there to protect them. Sometimes the soldiers have guard dogs, so tell your children not to touch these or any other strange animals.

There is usually a long wait for bags, at customs, at currency conversion and car rental counters, and at passport checkpoints. Explain this to your children before landing and tell them how much you appreciate their patience and good behavior. Saving some snacks for this long waiting period may be a good idea.

Going Home

As the time away from home winds down, remember to reconfirm all your return flight and airport shuttle van reservations twenty-four hours in advance—except in the cases of international travel, when you should do so seventy-two hours in advance. Give yourself enough time to get to the airport, return your car, and check in at least one hour before flight time.

On the way home from the airport, you might want to stop to pick up milk and any other perishables you will need your first morning home.

Book List

The following books about travel are suggested reading for you to share with your children. They are all appropriate for children ages three to six:

Anno's Journey
By Mitsumasa Anno
A wordless picture book that details a journey through Europe.

Emma's Vacation
By David McPhail
A true-to-life story about a vacationing family whose young daughter convinces them to stop sightseeing and to have fun sitting around together and relaxing.

First Flight
By David McPhail
The story of a young boy's first trip on an airplane.

Flying
By Gail Gibbons
A nonfiction book about the history of airplane travel,
with descriptions of different types of planes.

Checklist

Reservations
Plane
__Seat assignments
__Special meals

Accommodations
__Special rates
__Sleeping arrangements
__Children's activities
__Car seat

Getting Ready to Go
__Books about traveling by plane
__Brochures
__**My Disney Busy Bag** calendar

Talking to Children Before Trip
__Tour of airport

___Pictures of who you are going to visit

___Discussion of expectations of your visit

Packing
___Tote bags
___Clothes for layering
___Name tags inside and outside suitcase
___Blanket and favorite toy
___Prescription for glasses
___Night-light
___Wipes
___Snacks (crackers, small bags of pretzels, small boxes of cereal, cut-up fruit, boxed fruit juices, candy or gum to chew on during takeoff and landing)
___First aid kit (adhesive bandages, antibiotic ointment, thermometer, sunscreen, insect repellent, fever and pain relievers for both children and adults, medicines, and vitamins)

On the Plane
___Airplane rules
___Ears popping
___*Turbulence*

At the Destination
___Rest room
___Room safety
___Night-light
___Rules

International Travel
    ＿Blanket and favorite toy
    ＿Snacks for airport wait

Going Home
    ＿Discussion of trip/fun times
    ＿Market

Important Numbers

Airline phone numbers_______________________
Flight numbers ___________________________
____
____

Car rental agency phone numbers ___________
____
____

Confirmation numbers _____________________
____

Hotel (or other accommodations) phone
numbers _________________________________
____
____

Confirmation numbers _____________________
____
____
____

Family physician phone number _______________

Neighbors' phone numbers _______________

Automobile club phone number _______________
Other important phone numbers _______________

Month

Sunday	Monday	Tuesday	Wed

day	Thursday	Friday	Saturday